INSECTS UP CLOSE
Moths

by Patrick Perish

Note to Librarians, Teachers, and Parents:

Blastoff! Readers are carefully developed by literacy experts and combine standards-based content with developmentally appropriate text.

Level 1 provides the most support through repetition of high-frequency words, light text, predictable sentence patterns, and strong visual support.

Level 2 offers early readers a bit more challenge through varied simple sentences, increased text load, and less repetition of high-frequency words.

Level 3 advances early-fluent readers toward fluency through increased text and concept load, less reliance on visuals, longer sentences, and more literary language.

Level 4 builds reading stamina by providing more text per page, increased use of punctuation, greater variation in sentence patterns, and increasingly challenging vocabulary.

Level 5 encourages children to move from "learning to read" to "reading to learn" by providing even more text, varied writing styles, and less familiar topics.

Whichever book is right for your reader, Blastoff! Readers are the perfect books to build confidence and encourage a love of reading that will last a lifetime!

This edition first published in 2018 by Bellwether Media, Inc.

No part of this publication may be reproduced in whole or in part without written permission of the publisher. For information regarding permission, write to Bellwether Media, Inc., Attention: Permissions Department, 5357 Penn Avenue South, Minneapolis, MN 55419.

Library of Congress Cataloging-in-Publication Data

Names: Perish, Patrick, author.
Title: Moths / by Patrick Perish.
Description: Minneapolis, MN : Bellwether Media, Inc., 2018. | Series: Blastoff! Readers: Insects Up Close |
   Audience: Age 5-8. | Audience: K to Grade 3. | Includes bibliographical references and index.
Identifiers: LCCN 2017028792 | ISBN 9781626177185 (hardcover : alk. paper) | ISBN 9781681034119 (ebook)
Subjects: LCSH: Moths–Juvenile literature.
Classification: LCC QL544.2 .P474 2018 | DDC 595.78–dc23
LC record available at https://lccn.loc.gov/2017028792

Editor: Nathan Sommer   Designer: Steve Porter

Printed in the United States of America, North Mankato, MN.

Table of Contents

What Are Moths?

Moths have soft wings covered with **scales**. They are close family members to butterflies.

wing

scales

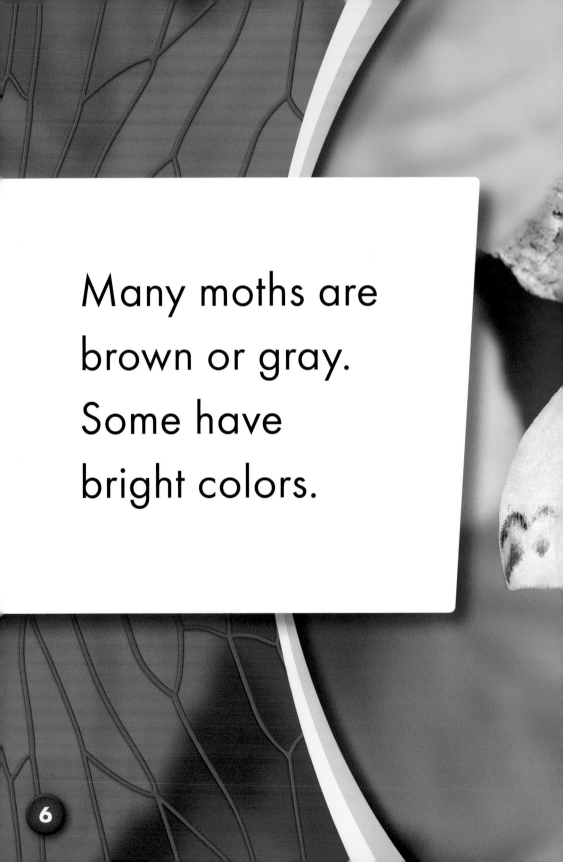

Many moths are
brown or gray.
Some have
bright colors.

ACTUAL
SIZE:
io moth

Big, feathery **antennae** help moths smell. They can smell things from miles away!

antennae

Moth Life

Moths live all over. They are often found in forests and grasslands.

11

Many moths
are **nocturnal**.
They come out
at night.

Moths have long, thin mouths. They use these to drink **nectar** from flowers.

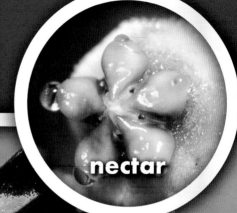

FAVORITE FOOD:

nectar

mouth

From Caterpillar to Moth!

Female moths lay their eggs on plants. **Caterpillars** break out of them.

eggs

Caterpillars eat leaves to grow. Soon, they spin silky **cocoons**.

caterpillars

**MOTH
LIFE SPAN:**
6 to 9 months

Caterpillars change inside their cocoons. Out come adults with brand new wings!

adult moth

cocoon

21

Glossary

antennae

feelers connected to the head that sense information around them

nectar

a sweet liquid that comes from plants, especially flowers

caterpillars

worm-like baby moths

nocturnal

active at night

cocoons

silk cases that moths spin around themselves for safety while they grow

scales

small plates that cover an animal's body

To Learn More

AT THE LIBRARY

Bodden, Valerie. *Moths*. Mankato, Minn.: Creative Education, 2014.

Coleman, Miriam. *Moths Drink Tears!* New York, N.Y.: PowerKids Press, 2014.

Rustad, Martha E. H. *Magnificent Moths*. North Mankato, Minn.: Capstone Press, 2017.

ON THE WEB

Learning more about moths is as easy as 1, 2, 3.

1. Go to www.factsurfer.com.

2. Enter "moths" into the search box.

3. Click the "Surf" button and you will see a list of related web sites.

With factsurfer.com, finding more information is just a click away.

Index

The images in this book are reproduced through the courtesy of: Cristian Gusa, front cover; ozgur kerem bulur, pp. 4-5; Cornel Constantin, p. 5 (inset); StevenRussellSmithPhotos, pp. 6-7, 10-11; Petlia Roman, pp. 6-7 (leaf foreground image); Alevanda, p. 7 (moth graphic); guraydere, pp. 8-9; Hailshadow, pp. 12-13; Tawansak, pp. 14-15; Srijira Ruechapaisarnanak, pp. 15 (inset), 22 (top right); Cathy Keifer, pp. 16-17; Hugh Lansdown, pp. 18-19; Trek13, pp. 20-21; SIMON SHIM (top left); Heather Hansen, p. 22 (center left); inlovepai, p. 22 (bottom left); Nuwat Phansuwan, p. 22 (center right); Nikola Rahme, p. 22 (bottom right).